AF434837

$$(w+o+r+d+s) = R_x$$

The Writing Code

Unlock the Secrets to Mental and Physical Wellbeing Through Writing

ARTHUR Q. GUTCH

An Imprint of ESOLO PRESS

Copyright © 2023 by Arthur Q. Gutch

Hardcover ISBN: 979-8-218-31034-9
Paperback ISBN: 979-8-218-31035-6

Printed in the United States of America

Published October 2023

Disclaimer

To everyone seeking to enhance their mental and physical well-being without breaking a sweat and to my family, friends and associates who have supported this journey.

Table of Contents

Note from the Author

Dear Readers,

I am thrilled to share with you what has become a lifelong journey through the world of words, books, and the untapped potential of writing in my latest work, *The Writing Code*. After more than a decade of collaborating with fellow writers, my passion for the written word and the entrepreneurial spirit has led me down an awe-inspiring path of discovery.

Throughout my life, I've been enamored by the enigmatic forces that underlie writing, learning, the wisdom of ancient civilizations and their hidden techniques for personal empowerment. This fascination has driven me to explore the uncharted territories of human potential, seeking to unravel the secrets that are embedded within the written word.

My heart resonates with the struggles faced by countless individuals battling mental and physical challenges. Recently, this has been amplified by the millions that continue to suffer the effects of the COVID 19 outbreak. This has fueled my determination to craft solutions that can bring relief to the lives of those in need. It is my belief that writing can be the next great exercise of the 21st century, guiding us towards health, well-being, and exceptional performance.

In the pursuit of this grand vision, with the help of others, at Lifewrite we are pioneering a revolutionary approach to harnessing the power of writing. This method has the potential to unlock wellness on a global scale, transforming lives of those that are suffering or seeking to level up. I believe we have the potential to reshape the landscape of personal wellness.

The synergy between human creativity and the marvels of AI has become a driving force behind my mission. By leveraging AI as a catalyst, we are propelling ourselves to new breakthroughs, ascending the ladder of health, well-being, and spiritual enlightenment.

As we delve deeper into this exploration, I am passionate about codifying the art and science of writing, forging a new paradigm for exercise - without breaking a sweat. It is my hope that *"The Writing Code"* will serve as a guide, empowering you to embark on a transformative journey that enhances every facet of your being.

With gratitude and excitement,

Arthur Q. Gutch

Introduction

The Power of Writing

While journaling has existed for years, guided, expressive writing enabled by AI with the purpose of leveling up or enhancing well-being in a measurable, transformational way is groundbreaking. It all started thousands of years ago and today has evolved to new heights of impact on our existence.

The History of Writing

Written language first emerged in 3000 BCE (or BC) in Mesopotamia, where it was used primarily for counting and accounting purposes. In the centuries since then, writing has evolved to not only play a pivotal role in long-distance communication and preservation of world history, but also in individual healing and self-actualization. Today, writing serves a greater purpose than it ever has before: it allows us to work through difficult emotions, approach life with purpose and intention, and improve our health and well-being.

The Neuroscience of Writing

You may consider speaking and writing one and the same or innately intertwined, but in actuality, the part of your brain that controls writing is separate from the part that controls speech. Researchers learned more about the separation between these two operations by studying patients recovering from a stroke: several who could speak but not write and one who could write but not speak. What they learned is that writing and speaking are different and separate operations, which may explain why writing has benefits that you cannot leverage through speaking.

From a neuroscientific perspective, writing provides two primary benefits over thinking or speaking when it comes to goals and working through difficult feelings. First, writing allows you to store your thoughts, ideas, and goals externally (on a hard drive or a piece of paper, for example). This ensures they exist somewhere other than your brain, which is fallible. Additionally, it gives you the opportunity to increase exposure by posting what you wrote in a conspicuous place, like the fridge or your bathroom mirror.

Second, writing improves the encoding process in your brain. Encoding is the process by which information travels to the hippocampus, a complex structure in the temporal lobe of your brain, to be analyzed. During analysis, your brain organizes information into two piles: keep and discard. Writing down your to-do list, goals, ideas, and realizations improves the likelihood that they will land in the "keep" pile and subsequently be stored in your long-term memory.

It is also important to note the generation effect phenomenon. Researchers have found that information is more likely to be stored, or remembered, when you have generated the idea or information yourself. That is, you are less likely to retain information you simply read than you are to retain information you generated. We can assume, then, that encoding is more successful when you are prompted to think through a complex situation than it is when you read a book or listen to a recorded meditation. Most people can recall at some point in their life when writing something down enabled them to better remember that information.

The Health Benefits of Writing

Half of all adults report that their stress has increased in the last year, and three-quarters report that they have experienced moderate or high stress levels in the last thirty days. Stress levels are rising in the workplace worldwide and stress levels among teens are a top concern for the American Psychological Association. Despite the tragic fact that depression is a leading cause of disability worldwide, less than 25% of people with depression will receive effective treatment.

Knowing how pervasive stress is around the globe is just one piece of the puzzle. Next, let's explore how stress impacts other aspects of health and wellness. According to the Mayo Clinic, stress has dramatic effects on one's behavior and mood. People who experience unhealthy stress (that is, long-term or episodic stress that begins to impact one's life in a negative way) might:

- overeat or undereat;

- use drugs, alcohol, or tobacco;

- withdraw from friends and family;

- experience angry outbursts;

- exercise less frequently;

- feel irritable, angry, sad, depressed, overwhelmed;

- have trouble focusing or getting motivated;

- experience anxiety and restlessness.

Additionally, stress can cause physical symptoms that make it difficult to do the things you enjoy (that might help you reduce stress levels). Physical symptoms of stress include chest pain, headache, fatigue, sleep disorders, muscle tension, pain, or reduced sex drive. Alarmingly, ongoing, poorly managed stress can cause serious and debilitating health problems like heart disease, high blood pressure, obesity, and diabetes.

Several studies conducted over the last two decades explore the relationship between expressive writing and health. According to Dr. John F. Evans in Psychology Today, expressive writing "Comes from our core. It is personal and emotional writing without regard to form or other writing conventions" like grammar and spelling. As an example, someone writing about a past trauma may pour out their deepest feelings about the experience and how it has impacted their life, including who they are and how they interact today with the people they love.

This kind of expressive writing can sometimes be uncomfortable, but studies demonstrate that it provides long-term benefits. Participants in expressive writing studies note that during the exercise, they feel heightened distress and physical symptoms. Long-term, however, they report both physical and social/behavioral improvements. Self-reported benefits include better mood, fewer depressive symptoms, a reduction in physical symptoms, and improved psychological well-being.

While these subjective measurements make the case for expressive writing on their own (who doesn't want to feel better, right?), these same studies also measured objective outcomes.

They found that those who consistently participate in expressive writing achieve improved blood pressure, lung function, and liver function. These individuals have fewer illness-related appointments, spend fewer days in the hospital, and achieve improved immune system functioning. Further, expressive writing contributes to higher grade-point averages, improved attendance at work, better memory, and stronger sporting performance.

Common Stress Management Techniques

A quick internet search reveals the prolific self-care options that exist for stress management. Some can be done at home with nothing but your mind, while others require specific equipment, products, or services. The trouble with what already exists is that it is exclusive; that is, not everybody can participate (and those suffering from debilitating depression and anxiety may be even less likely to participate because of their symptoms). Let's explore that:

- **Physical Exercise.** Studies demonstrate that exercise can have a profound effect on mental and physical health, but stress can cause aches and pains, obesity, and lack of motivation and focus - all of which make a regular exercise routine challenging if not out of reach for some people facing long-term stress.

- **Meditation.** Meditation refers to the practice of training our awareness and attention through mindfulness to achieve a calm state. Meditation is transformational for some people, while others find themselves unable to focus on a level that enables a positive impact. There is also a small group of people who experience unwanted effects like pain, anxiety symptoms, and depersonalization.

- **Journaling.** Journaling provides a wide range of health and wellness benefits ranging from improved immunity to reduced anxiety and more; however, to experience these benefits, it's important journaling not solely be used to vent but also to involve exploring thoughts and feelings more deeply. Anyone can write, even without a skill set in grammar and spelling; you do not have to be a good writer to realize the benefits of expressive writing.

- **Alternative Therapies.** There are myriad new age or alternative therapies designed to help you manage stress, but they have limitations, too. Most are expensive, so you must have the financial means to indulge. Most don't help you address or work through difficult feelings or emotions which cause stress in the first place. These modalities include Massage, Float Tanks, Salt Caves, Aromatherapy, etc.

The Solution: Guided Written Exercises

The prevalence of stress, anxiety, adult ADHD, and other challenges have increased over the last decade, but the American dream remains the same: self-reliance, freedom, equality, and an abundant life.

Everybody deserves access to the tools and resources they need to "level up" despite the obstacles along the course. At Lifewrite we are developing solutions that help you harness the power of writing to reach next-level health, wellness, well-being and achievement. Until now, expressive writing has been immeasurable. Lifewrite is codifying this methodology so you can measure your efforts and successes just like you would with a new fitness or weight-loss regimen.

Empowering you to direct your writing power to solve life's challenges and achieve improved physical and mental well-being is remarkable and the closest thing to magic!

CHAPTER 1

The History of Writing

Historically, we have used the written word to collect, store, manipulate, disseminate, retrieve, and communicate information. The characters or letters used have evolved over time, but so has how we use writing. Original uses included accounting and record-keeping, and while we still write for those purposes, we also now know that the power of writing far exceeds these initial purposes.

The Birth of the Written Word

The dramatic evolution might make it hard to believe, but today's written language is the direct descendant of the earliest forms of writing. What is most intriguing is that most researchers believe writing was independently invented at least four times throughout history in four different regions: Mesopotamia, Mesoamerica, Egypt, and China. Researchers believe that in each of these areas, writing was created from scratch, so to speak, with no prior knowledge of or exposure to cultures already using pictures and characters to communicate.

And yet the result in each area was relatively the same:

- First, characters used for accounting, to represent wages or transactions, for example - often tallies;

- Second, characters used to depict words, often a close replication of the visual representation (a simple bird shape for the word that means bird);

- Third, characters used to represent phonetic sounds and mimic spoken language, empowering people for the first time to write virtually anything they could say aloud.

Researchers believe that all written language evolved from these first four organic efforts or regions, including the words you are reading on this page, but it's important not to project our understanding of writing today on its role in these ancient cultures. The purpose and use of writing is vastly different today than in ancient times.

Ancient writing did not encourage literacy; that is, it was never intended for all of society. Instead, a select few highly skilled people learned how to write and read hieroglyphs or other forms of ancient writing, and anyone needing taxes calculated, for example, would seek out the help of a scribe. The average person would not have seen written language as relevant to their own lives; they would not have encountered or utilized writing in their daily lives.

Further, ancient writing was used by a select group of people for functional and spiritual purposes. Ancient cultures used writing to count, record transactions, record notable events, receive messages from God, and identify divine buildings, for example.

Writing was not used for creative or emotional expression or for the widespread sharing of information like it is today.

Communication Through Letter-Writing

Based on evidence available, historians believe the first hand-written letter was drafted around 500 B.C. by Persian Queen Atossa. While there is no record of the contents of her letter, it is often credited with introducing the genre of letter-writing world-wide.

Letters have been central to some of the most important moments in our world's history. Letters might include calls to action, documentation of historical events, or expression of love or other feelings. Some of the most influential letters written since that first letter include Dr. Martin Luther King's letter written from Birmingham Jail and Einstein's letter warning the U.S. administration of potential nuclear warfare, among others.

Letter writing has a rich history that spans across cultures and civilizations. Here is a brief overview of the evolution of letter writing in the world:

Ancient Civilizations

Mesopotamia (circa 3200 BCE - 539 BCE): One of the earliest recorded instances of letter writing comes from ancient Mesopotamia. Clay tablets were used to inscribe cuneiform script, contained distinct types of correspondence, including administrative messages and personal letters.

Egypt (circa 3100 BCE - 332 BCE): The ancient Egyptians also communicated through written messages, often on papyrus scrolls. These messages ranged from official decrees to personal letters and requests.

Classical Antiquity

Greece (8th century BCE - 6th century CE): Letter writing gained prominence in ancient Greece, with philosophers like Plato and Aristotle writing letters to their students and peers. Personal correspondence was highly valued, and letters were often exchanged among cities and individuals.

Rome (8th century BCE - 5th century CE): The Romans developed a sophisticated system of letter writing, known as "epistolography." Letters were essential for communication within the vast Roman Empire, ranging from official communications to intimate correspondence between friends and family.

Medieval and Renaissance Periods: Middle Ages (5th - 15th centuries CE) During the Middle Ages, letters played a crucial role in maintaining connections among individuals and institutions, particularly within the realm of religion, governance, and trade. Monasteries, scholars, and rulers exchanged letters to share knowledge and maintain alliances.

Renaissance (14th - 17th centuries): The Renaissance saw a revival of interest in classical letter writing. Intellectuals and humanists exchanged letters that discussed philosophical ideas, scientific discoveries, and artistic advancements. Letter writing became a form of intellectual exchange.

18th and 19th Centuries

Age of Enlightenment (18th century): The Enlightenment era saw the spread of ideas through letters, enabling philosophers and thinkers to share their perspectives on reason, liberty, and governance.

19th century: The development of more efficient postal systems led to a significant increase in personal letter writing. Letters became a primary means of long-distance communication, allowing people to stay connected despite physical distances.

20th Century and Beyond

Telegraph and Telephone Era: With the advent of the telegraph and telephone, the immediacy of communication changed. While letters remained important, faster modes of communication altered the dynamics of long-distance interactions.

Digital Age: The rise of email and other digital communication platforms in the late 20th and early 21st centuries transformed the way people communicate. While physical letter writing declined, digital correspondence allowed for instant communication on a global scale.

Throughout history, letter writing served as a means of personal expression, connection, diplomacy, trade, and the dissemination of knowledge. While the modes and methods of communication have evolved, the practice of letter writing continues to be a powerful way to convey thoughts, emotions, and information across time and space.

The Introduction of Expressive Writing

In the 1980s, researchers began exploring the concept of using writing for a new purpose: therapy. The findings of the first expressive writing study conducted were published in 1986. By 1997, additional studies had been conducted and a paper was published examining the relationship between expressive writing and both physical and biological outcomes based on evidence gathered across twenty different studies on the topic.

Some of these studies were revolutionary. While studying the therapeutic benefits of expressive writing, one researcher learned how debilitating keeping secrets about traumatic experiences could be on an individual's physical well-being. Through the course of his work, this researcher found that experiencing trauma was not necessarily the precursor to unwanted physical and emotional illness; rather, holding back thoughts, emotions, and behaviors surrounding the trauma was stressful in and of itself and likely to produce long-term problems requiring medical attention.

Overall, the string of studies conducted in the 1980s and 1990s found that writing about emotional experiences (as opposed to superficial topics) can be associated with 1) a reduction in physician visits, 2) improved immune system function including improved t-helper growth, 3) lower heart rate, 4) reduced phasic corrugator activity, and 5) long-term improvement in overall well-being and mood.

Prior to this research, writing served functional purposes like accounting, recordkeeping, and communication, but these novel studies changed the way psychologists, psychiatrists, and even individuals viewed writing. Although it would take some time to be widely adopted (and even today many do not know the long-term therapeutic benefits of writing), the written word serves a greater purpose today than perhaps ever before. As you continue reading, you will learn how to unleash the power of writing to apply these benefits to the obstacles and challenges you face in your own life.

Modern, expressive writing has become much more pervasive and based in scientific theory; however, its history is clear and summarized below:

Ancient Practices: Ancient Egyptians engaged in "negative confession," writing regrets and emotions on papyrus. Greeks and Romans used writing for reflection, personal communication, and philosophical discourse.

Medieval and Renaissance Periods: Medieval diaries and personal accounts provided insights into emotions and experiences. Renaissance humanists exchanged letters to share intellectual ideas and emotions.

Cultural Context: Jewish tradition included prayer, personal reflection, and interpretation in writings. Diaries documented Jewish experiences, including Anne Frank's during the Holocaust.

Modern Approaches: Sigmund Freud incorporated writing in psychoanalysis for self-expression. James Pennebaker's research in the 20th century highlighted therapeutic benefits of writing.

Evolution over Time: Expressive writing has adapted to changing communication technologies, from ancient tablets to digital platforms.

Throughout history, expressive writing has been a powerful tool for processing emotions, seeking self-understanding, and sharing thoughts, fostering both personal growth and connections within societies.

Social Media's Contributions

Although social media is often associated with negative consequences for mental health, its story is intimately intertwined with ours and important to explore here. Let's first consider the definition of social media according to Merriam Webster: "forms of electronic communication (such as websites for social networking and microblogging) through which users create online communities to share information, ideas, personal messages, and other content (such as videos)." With that definition in mind, the earliest forms of social media were email, chat rooms, online bulletin boards, and instant messaging introduced in the nineties.

Blogs quickly followed before social media as we know it today was born:

- LinkedIn in 2002;

- MySpace in 2003;

- Facebook in 2004;

- Reddit and YouTube in 2005;

- Twitter in 2006;

- Instagram and Pinterest in 2010;

- Snapchat in 2011;

- TikTok in 2016.

Social media quickly grew in popularity and today, 72% of adults are on social media. The most popular is Instagram, followed by YouTube and Snapchat. With social media, everybody has an audience for the written word - a place to share questions, worries, achievements, stories, or experiences. In the race for likes, shares, and genuine connection, people who never would have written a word in their lives (except what's required) *do* write on social media.

However, using social media as our primary avenue for expressive writing can be dangerous. Studies have linked heavy social media use with higher risk of anxiety, depression, self-harm, loneliness, and suicidal thoughts. Furthermore, studies have found that being exposed to traumatic events through social media can have the same devastating effects as being exposed to the event first-hand: higher stress, post-traumatic stress symptoms, and increased physical illnesses and ailments over time. Having a private space in which to share difficult thoughts and feelings through expressive writing is important. Despite the satisfaction that might accompany likes and shares on social media, the damage that can come from heavy social media use or rejection and hurtful comments is greater.

From Therapy to Personal Wellness

Therapeutic, expressive writing in its current form was nonexistent before the 1980s and has been reserved for use by professionals since then.

But the truth is billions of people are engaging in expressive writing every day through social media, and **anybody can unlock the power of expressive writing from the safety of their own home.** These exercises *do not* have to be led by a psychiatrist in an exam room to be effective; in fact, they are most effective when done often and privately, as long as you focus on your thoughts and feelings throughout the process.

Guided writing exercises developed according to evidence can help you unlock the power of expressive writing and codify the process so you can measure your growth over time. What is holding you back?

CHAPTER 2

The Neuroscience of Writing

In the first chapter, you learned that writing and speaking are housed in different parts of the brain and that separation between the two exists as evidenced by patients recovering from a stroke who lost one function but not the other. You also learned about the benefits of writing over speech: external storage and improved encoding, both of which translate to improved memory and results. One of the reasons behind the improvement in encoding - or committing to memory - is the generation effect: information is more likely to be committed to memory when you generate it yourself than it is when you simply hear it or read it.

It can be hard to imagine that writing could ever be quantified or 'codified' in the same way that exercise can; it cannot be measured in reps, miles, or pounds. However, prolific studies on the way the brain behaves during a writing exercise - especially when writing about negative experiences and emotions - exist. By leveraging everything we have learned through historical studies, we can codify the benefits of writing for the first time in history.

In this chapter, we will explore the neuroscience of writing to build further understanding of what happens in the brain when pen meets paper.

Introduction to the Brain

Your brain is comprised of three parts: the cerebrum, the cerebellum, and the brain stem. The cerebrum, the largest and outermost part of the brain, is divided into four lobes:

- frontal, which is responsible for voluntary movement, producing language, higher-level thinking like problem-solving, planning, and judgment, and personality, including social behavior, emotions, and impulse control;

- parietal, which interprets touch, position in space, and taste;

- temporal, responsible for understanding language, memory, hearing, and smell, and;

- occipital, which is responsible for vision.

The cerebellum is just below the cerebrum and controls posture, coordination, and balance. The brainstem, at the bottom of the brain and connecting to the spinal cord, drives autonomic processes like heart rate, breathing, and sleeping.

All the complex functions controlled by the brain rely on neural pathways, or connections between two or more neurons. You have neural pathways established at this moment, but your brain is both flexible and adaptable, which means you can change, add, and strengthen pathways all the time.

Neural pathways can be likened to a trail. When you take the same path through woods many times, a trail forms and it gets easier and easier to take that path in the future. Likewise, when you spiral into negative thoughts every time you think about going to work, for example, a pathway is strengthened. Next time you think about work, the 'trail' with the fewest barriers leads you to spiraling into negative thoughts.

If you change your path through the woods, the old trail will be overtaken by trees and grass, making it more difficult to travel. The new trail will become the path of least resistance as vegetation clears and a path begins to form. Neural pathways are similar; you can retrain your brain to develop new pathways simply by going down that road - thinking in a new way and doing so repetitively.

Cognitive Load

The human brain is inundated with information every moment of every day. Consider paying for your coffee at the drive through. Your foot is on the brake of your car, so you do not drive away. A landscaper mows a lawn in the background. The baristas are chatting with one another and with you. Your podcast is playing over Bluetooth, periodically interrupted by notifications: a new email, a like on Instagram, a comment on Facebook. Espresso machines are hissing from within the building. There are children or dogs in the backseat of your car, lively and boisterous. Somewhere, a car honks while cool air from the air conditioning blasts on your face.

This information is first received by your sensory memory, which discards information that is not useful. In this case, your sensory memory ensures the baristas' background conversations, and the running lawnmower do not take the brain space you need to keep your foot on the brake and make your payment.

This is where cognitive load comes in, by managing the amount of information working memory can hold at once. Information that makes it through the sensory memory reaches the working memory. Your working memory can manage five to nine pieces of information at a time, and from there selected items are encoded - or stored to your long-term memory - and others are discarded. One way to help ensure information is encoded rather than cast-off is to write it down: information you generate, or make up yourself, and information you write down are more likely to be stored in your long-term memory. This is especially helpful when goalsetting.

The Impact of Writing on Brain Activity

With this understanding of the brain, we can begin to break down what happens in this fascinating organ when you write.

Consider the impact of a high-intensity workout on your body: your muscles are burning from your core to your calves (maybe beyond), sweat is running into your eyes, and your heart and lungs are engaged at max capacity. Writing is for your brain what bootcamp is for your body: strenuous and stimulating exercise. In fact, the entire time you are writing - especially something you have never written before, or a first draft - nearly every part of the brain continues working at that capacity, establishing brand new neural connections or pathways in the brain.

As a result of this strenuous mental exercise, you develop new organizational skills, increase your ability to reason and solve problems, and expand your vocabulary.

Expressive Writing and the Brain

While the outcomes above come from writing in any form (letters, journaling, creative writing - even homework), expressive writing affects the brain in a unique and fascinating way.

As a reminder, expressive writing refers to personal, emotional writing that may not adhere to the typical rules, like spelling, grammar, and punctuation. You can engage in an expressive writing exercise about anything:

- a traumatic experience in your past;

- a conversation that did not go as planned today;

- things that make you happy;

- a favorite memory and what you heard, saw, smelled, and felt in that moment;

- a big goal;

- a recent achievement;

- a relationship that is becoming challenging or painful for you

- a grudge.

Expressive writing has clear and measurable results because it leads to the formation of new neural pathways. Consider first a routine negative experience, like receiving corrections at work. Prior to expressive writing, perhaps the thought process based on the most comfortable neural pathways looked something like this:

- "I did the best I could, and it isn't good enough. I'll never be good enough."

- "I fail at everything I try."

- "Why me? Why do all the bad things happen to me?"

- "After all I've done for them, they treat me like this? They don't value me at all."

- "She obviously thinks I'm worthless."

- "I *am* worthless."

Expressive writing can help you release all those feelings and build new pathways by exploring other perspectives. While those old paths were likely well-worn, your brain is flexible. New paths revealed through expressive writing might look something like this:

- "My manager sees my potential and is committed to helping me achieve it."

- "I'm glad I know exactly what's expected of me so I can meet and exceed expectations."

- "If I can overcome this, my leader will see that I'm coachable and determined."

- "This experience is helping me improve."

The first time you try this, a new neural pathway is created. Like a trail, the old pathway is still better worn, so you will default to that old pathway instead of the new pathway the next time you face similar adversity. But each time you make the effort to engage in the expressive writing exercise, you make the new path easier and easier to travel. Soon, you will default to this pathway when you face new struggles. According to research, if you engage in expressive writing just three times a week for twenty minutes a day, you can expect to see a change in thoughts and behavior. In this case, the result would be a more positive and helpful response to difficult feedback.

All of this information supports the necessity for **guided,** expressive writing. If you use expressive writing as a venting session and then 'hang up your pen,' those harmful neural pathways are reinforced. The same trail taken repeatedly makes it the easiest trail next time, resulting in habitual negative thoughts and behaviors.

However, when expressive writing is used as a way to explore and reframe difficult thoughts and feelings - through prompting and guiding - new pathways are created. These pathways are more conducive to a happy and successful life, and consistent expressive writing can quickly lead to not only forming these new paths but 'wearing' the trail, resulting in habitual, positive, and productive thoughts and behaviors.

Additionally, as mentioned before, expressive writing improves encoding for two reasons: it offers external storage (someplace to store the information aside from your brain, reducing the impact of cognitive load), and you are generating the information yourself instead of reading what someone else has written.

Codifying Expressive Writing for Total Transformation

That is it! That is the neuroscience behind expressive writing. With that understanding, it suddenly becomes easier to realize how expressive writing can be transformational for *anyone* and how you can measure both the effort and results of expressive writing.

Because expressive writing exercises every part of your brain, it lets you take control of what is committed to long-term memory, and facilitates the creation of new, more productive, neural pathways. As a result, it is incredibly beneficial for:

- Reframing stressors to impact you less;

- Setting and achieving ambitious goals (the kind that others might call crazy);

- Enhancing your performance at work and at home;

- Changing your habits to better serve you;

- Working through demanding situations, thoughts, and feelings;

- Understanding and navigating challenging relationships;

- Healing from traumatic experiences.

Writing with intention is a **measurable** way to transform your life. Just like you might know how much water you should drink in a day to reach your health goals, research and neuroscience tell us exactly how often you should participate in expressive writing, what those exercises should look like to be effective, and how this can change the way your brain functions.

We call this codifying writing to unlock its power for healing and whole life transformation, and Lifewrite is on a mission to *master* it.

CHAPTER 3

Stress in Today's World

We are not facing the same problems today that our ancestors faced, so we cannot cope with our challenges in the same ways that our ancestors did. While there is always learning available from the past, sometimes we must reinvent the wheel in order to adapt in a changing world. In this chapter, we explore evolution as it relates to stress and fight or flight mode, as well as societal impact on stress.

Evolution and Stress

Stress does play a specific role in our bodies: many (many) years ago, it was fear and adrenaline that kept those who came before us out of the mouths of wolves and safe from other precarious situations. Today, healthy stress helps us respond quickly in dangerous situations. When we feel stress, act, and experience an immediate return, fear and worry are helpful. Consider these examples:

- You notice a car veering into your lane. You feel panic and move into action, honking, slowing, and moving onto the shoulder. As a result, the other driver looks up and corrects his vehicle. You are safe and your stress is resolved.

- While walking your dog, you notice a rattlesnake in the tall grass. You feel immediate fear and guide your dog back in the direction you came from. As a result, you and your dog are safe.

- While pushing the shopping cart through Target, your toddler wiggles her way out of the seatbelt and stands up. After an immediate wave of fear, you move with cat-like reflexes to catch her before she falls and gets hurt. Baby is okay because stress drove intervention - quickly and effectively.

All of these situations produced an immediate return: situation > stress > action > positive result. However, the stress our bodies were designed to experience as a safety mechanism can quickly become debilitating when applied to situations with a delayed return.

Why is that a problem? Because the *vast majority* of stress you and I experience on a daily basis is not about the present moment. That means most of the stress the average American experiences on a daily basis is *unhealthy* and *chronic*. It does not visit for a fleeting moment and then pass when the crisis is averted; it persists because the return is delayed. Consider these examples:

- You log into your retirement planning website at work and see that the amount you have saved and the amount you should have saved by now are vastly different...and not in your favor. You worry that you will not have enough saved for retirement.

- Your doctor tells you that you are overweight and shares the prognosis. You are at higher risk of developing myriad serious and life-threatening conditions. You begin to worry that you will not live a long, quality life.

- You spent the evening with friends and said something that was not well-received by the group. You get home and replay it in your mind over and over again, asking yourself, 'Why did I say that?' and *What was I thinking?'* You begin to wonder if they are talking about you, what they think of you, and if they will ever want to hang out with you again.

This is where evolution has not quite caught up yet. While we could benefit from evolutionary changes right about now - particularly some adaptations to stress in delayed-return situations - evolution is slow. For around 200,000 years, the way our bodies reacted to stress served us well. Now, society has shifted. The way we think and behave has shifted. And all of that has happened in just five hundred years, or 2.5% of the previous 'era.'

While we are waiting for evolution to address the problems associated with nearly constant fight-or-flight stress and rare immediate return, there are steps we can take today to help manage our stress levels despite the way our bodies function. One of the most helpful steps is shifting our focus from a problem that is far away (in the past or the future) to a problem we can solve today that serves as a steppingstone to solving the bigger problem.

From the scenarios above, it might look something like this:

- Instead of worrying about whether you will be able to retire someday, increase your retirement allocation by 1% today.

- Instead of worrying about your weight, take a walk or add a vegetable to your dinner today.

- Instead of worrying about what your friends think of you, send a quick text to convey your intentions and get the reassurance you need.

Guided writing helps the participant shift their focus from big, impossible, and far away to here, now, and within reach. It can help with work-related stress, relationship issues, parenting, academic pressures, health concerns, financial worries, family challenges, grief, anxiety, personal growth, and everyday frustrations. The goal is to process emotions, gain insights, and improve overall well-being. It's not about perfect writing but about self-expression!

Societal Impact on Stress

Now that we have explored the impact of stress on our brain and how our brain processes these worrisome situations, it is also important to understand how external factors play a role.

The American Psychological Association conducts an annual poll to evaluate stress levels in America. Their 2022 poll, conducted in February and March, revealed that Americans are 'besieged by stress.' Furthermore, they found that for the first time in known history, as many as 80% of Americans cite the same sources for their stress, which means there are new stressors impacting nearly the entire nation instead of just individual stressors like divorce, health problems, and financial strain. Even more concerning is that many Americans reported being in this 'fight or flight' mode for years now without a break. The stressors cited in the survey included:

- worry following the two-year COVID-19 pandemic and the impact it had on their personal lives, professional lives, and families;

- stress about inflation, especially as it is impacting everyday items like gas and groceries;

- fear surrounding the invasion of Ukraine and what it means for those directly impacted as well as the rest of the world; many worried that America was at risk for aiding Ukraine or that these attacks mark the beginning of World War III;

- the worry parents carry that their children's social, emotional, and academic development was impacted by the COVID-19 pandemic.

This stress has wreaked physical havoc on its hosts, too, in the form of health problems, aches and pains, and weight gain. This means that this relentless stress is not limited to those who have mental health diagnoses; *nearly everyone* reports chronic and debilitating stress. Whether you are happy, sad, successful, or waiting for your moment, finding healthy ways to cope with difficult thoughts, feelings, and situations will be imperative to bridge the gap between our physiology and the stressors of today's world.

When it comes to bona fide mental health disorders, statistics are alarming:

- Almost 50 million adults in America experienced mental illness in 2019 alone; that is almost 20% of all adults;

- The percentage of adults who have had serious thoughts of suicide has increased every single year since 2012; it is up to 4.58% percent;

- In the last year, 15% of our youth experienced a major depressive episode, while rates increased by 52% between 2005 and 2017;

- Over half of all adults with a mental illness receive no treatment at all;

- Over 60% of the youth in America experiencing major depression have never received any medical treatment;

- Among the youth who do receive treatment for severe depression, less than a third receive consistent care.

It is important to note that those with anxiety are often at higher risk of developing other disorders. The most common conditions that exist alongside anxiety are major depressive disorder, substance use disorder, and bipolar disorder.

Finally, you may wonder where social media comes in when discussing the societal impact on stress. The answer is, it both helps and hurts. Studies have demonstrated that personal connection through social media can improve well-being. Examples include a direct message from a close friend or a positive comment from someone you care about on a photo you posted. It also provides a community for those experiencing problems with their mental and physical health, allowing them to connect with others like them, share tips and tricks, and encourage one another. During COVID-19, social media provided a platform for human interaction when it was difficult to attain this in the 'real world.'

However, the same studies show that these benefits diminish the more time you spend on social media. Using social media platforms more than two hours a day can increase feelings of social isolation, increase the incidence of depression, and increase the likelihood of experiencing anxiety symptoms or developing an anxiety disorder.

Directing Your Own Future

It is easy to get bogged down with the challenges and problems of today, but there is much you can do to increase your outcomes. We will dive deeper into future chapters but battling chronic worry in a delayed-return era with both tragic and worrisome worldwide events requires intention and effort. It requires you to spend a little more time exploring your thoughts and feelings around demanding situations and reframing them in a way that is productive and conducive to the today and tomorrow you hope to build. It requires establishing micro-habits to reduce stress, improve clarity, and set goals.

Guided, expressive writing is an incredibly effortless way to do all these things from the comfort of your own home, while measuring both your effort and results, much like diet and exercise.

CHAPTER 4

Finding Meaning in Life

Just like stress, the search for meaning in life can be helpful or cause great pain and strain in your life. **Hear us out - this chapter has a happy conclusion.**

Whether the search for meaning is helpful or painful can depend on the stage or phase of life you are in, but it can also depend on how you approach it. An intentional, mindful approach to finding meaning can help you live knowing that your actions and decisions make a real difference in the world. An intentional, mindful approach can help you live knowing that your life matters. That *you* matter.

Finding Meaning and Purpose

Your meaning and purpose in life can feel like a secretive concept that only philosophers have unlocked. You can find all the information you need when it comes to career, relationship, money, and wellness, but meaning is much more challenging to research in a scientific way. The deeper you dig through the archives of research and information online, the more complex and conflicting information you will find. Instead of leaving enlightened, you are likely to leave deflated.

Why is that? For centuries, we have attached **enormous gravity** to the meaning of life. We wonder who created us and why, what purpose we were created to fulfill and how we will know when we fulfill it, and more. Discovering why we are here and what we are called to do with the life we have been entrusted with has been left up to philosophers and scholars - and even *they* do not agree on the answers to those questions. Yet, the desire to live a meaningful and purposeful life remains. Our greatest fear (and perhaps greatest source of delayed return stress) stays the same: we worry that we are insignificant in the big picture, that everything we have done in our time here does not matter...and therefore *we* don't matter.

Without purpose, our daily lives can feel aimless. Why take the stairs instead of the elevator? Why give instead of spend? Why have children when you can live for yourself? Making daily decisions that are meaningful and beneficial depends upon a sense of purpose.

In this chapter, we will crack the code of meaning and purpose so you can discover your own. With a better understanding of your purpose, you can become the author of your own life, one experience and one decision at a time.

A Shift in Perspective

Research has shown that stress is highest among those who are looking for meaning and purpose in their lives and lowest among those who feel their lives have meaning and purpose already.

Studies have also found that those who are young (in their twenties) and those who are older (retired with adult children, for example) are most likely to be in the 'searching for meaning' stage, while those who are middle-aged are most likely to have found meaning in their daily lives.

What does that mean?

Two things: Stop looking for the meaning of life and find meaning and purpose in the life you already have. What's interesting about the u-shaped curve mentioned above is that those who once 'knew' the meaning of life can lose that as they age and their roles change. Those in their twenties who aren't sure about their career or life partner yet are searching for meaning; those who are middle-aged, dedicated to a career, a partner, and often children have a strong sense of meaning; and those who are retired and empty nesters begin to search for meaning again. That indicates that finding meaning and purpose is less about unlocking ancient secrets and more about *the things we do* every single day. The mundane. The small. The seemingly insignificant.

It indicates that perhaps making a cup of coffee for your partner, doing work that you love, taking a hike while the sun rises, or rocking a baby to sleep *are* the meaning of life. Perhaps we are missing out on the meaning of life because we're wasting our time searching for it.

So how do you stop searching and start finding purpose in the life you already have?

It is easier than you might think. It does not require you to give up your worldly possessions, quit your job, or join a monastery. It simply requires you to 1) be more mindful of the unimportant things, 2) establish positive habits and routines, and 3) share your gifts with others.

Be More Mindful

Mindfulness is one effortless way to be more present and more aware and appreciative of the small things. Some ways to increase your mindfulness include:

- **Pause.** Avoid the temptation to fill every moment of your life with activity. Instead, pause sometimes and take in your surroundings: what do you see, hear, smell, and feel? Sometimes the most indulgent, joyful moments are the simplest - a hot shower, a new flower opening, the first sip of coffee, or a touch from someone you love.

- **Breathe deeply.** Pay attention only to your breath while breathing deeply in and out, in and out. Do this when you feel anxious, overwhelmed, or tired.

- **Explore.** Explore and identify your emotions. Ask yourself what emotion you are feeling and why you are feeling that way.

- **Reflect.** Take time to reflect on the good. What went well today? What did you learn today? How did you grow today? What did you do for yourself and others today?

- **Write.** Expressive or guided writing can help us take a more mindful look at our thoughts, feelings, and experiences, exploring the good and extracting learnings from them.

Enhancing mindfulness through writing is a powerful and introspective practice that can help you cultivate a deeper awareness of your thoughts, emotions, and experiences. This process involves intentionally engaging in writing activities that promote self-reflection, presence, and an overall sense of mindfulness.

Here's a list of writing techniques to enhance mindfulness through writing:

- *Set an Intention:* Begin by setting a clear intention for your writing practice. Decide what aspect of mindfulness you want to focus on – it could be observing your thoughts without judgment, being present in the moment, or exploring your emotions.

- *Choose a Writing Space*: Find a quiet and cozy space where you can write without distractions. This will help you immerse yourself fully in the writing process.

- *Freewriting*: Start with freewriting – a technique where you write whatever comes to mind without censoring or judging your thoughts. This practice encourages you to let go of any inhibitions and express yourself freely.

- *Stream of Consciousness*: Write in a stream-of-consciousness style. Allow your thoughts to flow naturally, without trying to structure or organize them. This mimics the flow of your mind and encourages you to observe your thoughts as they arise.

- *Mindful Descriptions*: Engage your senses in your writing. Describe your surroundings, feelings, and experiences in detail. This brings your attention to the present moment and grounds you in your immediate environment.

- *Gratitude Journaling*: Write about things for which you are grateful. This practice encourages you to focus on positive aspects of your life, promoting a sense of contentment and appreciation in the present moment.

- *Emotional Exploration*: Write about your emotions without judgment. If you're feeling stressed, anxious, or happy, describe these emotions and their physical sensations. This helps you acknowledge and process your feelings mindfully.

- *Thought Observation*: Practice observing your thoughts without attachment. Write down your thoughts as if you're an impartial observer. This can create distance between you and your thoughts, reducing their impact on your emotions.

- *Reflective Journaling*: Set aside time each day to reflect on your experiences, observations, and interactions. Write about what you've learned, what challenged you, and how you responded mindfully.

- *Self-Compassion Writing*: Practice self-compassion by writing a supportive and kind letter to yourself. Treat yourself with the same empathy you would offer to a friend facing the same type of situation.

- *Reread and Reflect*: After writing, take some time to reread what you've written. Reflect on the insights you've gained, any patterns you've noticed, and how the writing process itself felt.

Remember, the goal of enhancing mindfulness through writing is not to produce perfect prose, but to connect with your thoughts and experiences in a nonjudgmental and present-focused way. Over time, this practice can lead to a heightened sense of self-awareness, emotional regulation, and a deeper understanding of your inner landscape.

Establish Positive Habits

Research demonstrates that the more we *think* about the meaning of life, the less meaning we have in our lives. Overthinking is paralyzing, and in the worst cases, can make even the simplest daily tasks, like bathing, feel like impossible feats.

The best way to spend less time thinking about meaning is to spend more time doing the things that bring meaning and purpose into your life. And the best way to do that is to establish positive habits and routines.

The quickest way to go wrong is to start too big. Maybe you want to live a meaningful life, so you decide to cure cancer. But the pressure of having to cure cancer is paralyzing. Not only do you never cure cancer, but you also actually never get out of bed because you're paralyzed by the pressure of having to cure cancer or the fear of failure when you do try.

The most successful way to cure cancer is to ask yourself, "What single thing can I do in this moment?" And then, it might look something like this: get out of bed. In the next moment, perhaps you brush your teeth. In the next moment, maybe you eat a healthy breakfast to nourish your body. And *then,* in that *next* moment, maybe you explore biology degrees at your local university. Maybe that's as far as you get today. **Four steps further** than never getting out of bed.

All success begins with positive habits. And positive habits usually begin with a list of what we like to call micro habits: things that can be done in a moment that, when done consistently, lead to health and happiness. They include health, hygiene, reflection, giving, and doing. They are actions and they work. And they all start with writing.

Share Your Gifts with Others

Pablo Picasso said, "The meaning of life is to find your gift. The purpose of life is to give it away." This might mean being a great friend, making people laugh, raising children, curing cancer, or being the greatest street sweeper who ever lived.

Sharing your writing with others can offer several benefits:

- *Validation and Connection*: When you share your thoughts and feelings with others, it can validate your experiences and emotions. Knowing that others can relate to what you're going through can create a sense of connection and reduce feelings of isolation.

- *Different Perspectives*: Others may provide fresh perspectives and insights on your writing. They might offer alternative viewpoints that you hadn't considered, helping you gain a deeper understanding of your own thoughts and feelings.

- *Feedback and Improvement*: Constructive feedback from others can help you refine your writing skills. Whether it's grammar and style suggestions or comments on the content, feedback can assist you in becoming a better writer.

- *Emotional Release*: Sharing your writing can be cathartic, especially when discussing personal struggles or emotions. Expressing your feelings openly can help release pent-up emotions and alleviate stress.

- *Support and Encouragement*: People who care about you can offer emotional support and encouragement. Their words can provide a sense of comfort and motivation to keep writing and working through your challenges.

- *Empowerment*: Sharing your writing requires vulnerability, which can lead to a sense of empowerment. It takes courage to open up to others, and doing so can boost your confidence and self-esteem.

- *Social Interaction*: Sharing your writing can trigger conversations and discussions about important topics. These interactions can expand your social circle, foster deeper relationships, and create meaningful connections.

- *Awareness and Reflection*: Explaining your thoughts to others can help you articulate your feelings more clearly. This process of explaining can generate greater self-awareness and insights into your own experiences.

- *Inspiration to Others*: Your writing might resonate with others who are going through similar challenges. By sharing your experiences, you could inspire and provide comfort to those who are facing similar situations.

- *Creativity and Inspiration*: Seeing how others react to your writing can spark innovative ideas and creativity. The interaction between your words and their responses can lead to innovative thinking and new directions for your writing.

Not all writing needs to be shared, especially if it's deeply personal or sensitive. If you choose to share your writing, make sure you're sharing with individuals you trust and in environments that feel safe.

CHAPTER 5

A Discussion on Modern-Day Treatment

Now that we have explored the problems stress and the search for meaning can present in our lives, let us explore how modern society addresses those problems: through interventions like self-care, meditation, medication, yoga, journaling, and exercise. All of these solutions are right for some people, but each has limitations that require consideration when determining best fit for you.

Self-Care

Origins of the self-care movement have ancient roots, appearing in various forms in distinct cultures throughout history. Practices related to self-care, such as meditation, herbal remedies, and rituals for physical and mental well-being can be found in ancient civilizations like the Egyptians, Greeks, and Romans. Self-care grew from various historical and cultural influences. It gained prominence through second-wave feminism, mental health advocacy, rejection of consumerism, and the rise of social media. Audre Lorde's Black feminist perspective and the wellness industry also contributed. The movement emphasizes prioritizing personal well-being, especially in the digital age, while acknowledging diversity and individual identities. Self-care encompasses a broad range of practices and encourages intentional actions for holistic health and self-compassion.

One look at society and social media today will tell you that self-care is about:

- candle-lit bubble baths with a glass of wine and a good book;

- sleeping in on a Saturday morning;

- indulging in the finer things like massages, and spa days;

- seeking out a new trail to hike and enjoy the outdoors;

- time alone without responsibility;

- saying no and setting personal boundaries.

There *is* good that has stemmed from today's understanding of self-care. People have become more comfortable setting boundaries when it comes to their bodies. Employees have become more comfortable prioritizing the areas of their life that are not work. We have all become more familiar with our limits and made conscientious and intentional decisions regarding where we focus our time and efforts.

However, today's version of self-care as a response to stress and search for meaning has shortcomings. Nearly every religion in the world agrees that service to others is the greatest form of self-care, providing physical, mental, and emotional benefits that can't be replaced by bubble baths and alone time. The more we say no to the things that serve others and yes to the things that serve the 'self,' the more we miss the benefits of doing good. In trying to become whole, we may be losing more than we gain.

Additionally, many forms of self-care have been commercialized and monetized, which means you often have to spend money in order to engage in self-care. Subsequently, the search for stress relief becomes expensive. For many people, it leads to living beyond their means and contributes to larger financial problems and long-term stress – the exact dilemma they were hoping to escape in the first place.

Exercise

Exercise is perhaps the best modern solution to stress, anxiety, and search for meaning (aside from what we're about to share with you, but we'll save that for the next chapter).

You can exercise without setting any time aside at all. Consider these possibilities: park in the furthest spot in the parking lot at work, take the stairs instead of the elevator, and walk to the mailbox instead of pulling over as you drive past it each day,

You can exercise while experiencing nature: hike through the forest, enjoying the wildflowers and singing birds; bike through your neighborhood, taking in the smells of Fall; or swim in the lake nearby, feeling the cold water against your skin.

You can exercise socially: join group fitness classes at your local gym, participate in a fundraiser 5k with friends and family, or help a friend landscape their yard on the weekend.

Exercise comes in so many varieties and modifications that it can be done anywhere for any length of time with no equipment at all. It improves weight, brain health, bone and muscle strength, and ability to participate in everyday activities. Frequent exercise improves mental health and reduces your risk of disease.

However, some people experience limitations due to reduced range of motion, pain, muscle wasting, or reduction in strength. In addition, while exercise has a positive impact on mental health, it does nothing to help you work through difficult thoughts, feelings, and situations in an intentional and action-driven way.

Listed below are some of the risks and benefits of exercise for mental and physical well-being:

Benefits:

Improved Mood: Exercise is known to release endorphins, which are often referred to as "feel-good" hormones. This can lead to an improved mood and reduced feelings of stress and anxiety.

Stress Reduction: Regular physical activity can help reduce the body's stress response by promoting relaxation and lowering stress hormones like cortisol.

Enhanced Cognitive Function: Exercise has been linked to improved cognitive functions such as memory, attention, and problem-solving. It can also reduce the risk of cognitive decline with age.

Boosted Self-Esteem: Achieving fitness goals and seeing physical improvements can boost self-esteem and self-confidence.

Better Sleep: Regular exercise can improve the quality and duration of sleep, leading to better overall rest and rejuvenation.

Weight Management: Engaging in regular physical activity can help maintain a healthy weight or support weight loss efforts.

Cardiovascular Health: Exercise strengthens the heart and improves blood circulation, reducing the risk of cardiovascular diseases like heart attacks and strokes.

Muscle and Bone Strength: Weight-bearing exercises, such as resistance training, can increase muscle mass and bone density, reducing the risk of osteoporosis and fractures.

Improved Immune Function: Moderate exercise can enhance immune system function, making your body more resilient to illnesses.

Social Interaction: Participating in group exercises or team sports can provide opportunities for social interaction and help combat feelings of loneliness.

Limitations:

Overexertion and Injury: Pushing yourself too hard or performing exercises with improper form can lead to injuries such as strains, sprains, and fractures.

Health Conditions: Certain health conditions may be exacerbated by intense exercise. It's important to consult a healthcare professional before starting a new exercise regimen, especially if you have chronic health conditions.

Burnout: Overtraining without proper rest and recovery can lead to physical and mental burnout, negatively affecting your well-being.

Mental Health Concerns: While exercise can improve mental health, excessive exercise or a compulsion to exercise can become problematic, leading to conditions like exercise addiction or body dysmorphia.

Comparative Stress: Comparing oneself to others in fitness settings can lead to feelings of inadequacy and stress.

Time Commitment: Finding time for regular exercise can be challenging, especially for individuals with busy schedules.

Physical Demands: Some forms of exercise might be physically demanding, making them unsuitable for individuals with certain health conditions or physical limitations.

Dehydration and Exhaustion: Not hydrating properly during exercise can lead to dehydration, and excessive exertion without proper fueling can result in exhaustion.

Pressure and Expectations: Pressure to achieve certain fitness goals or conform to specific body standards can lead to psychological stress.

Inadequate Guidance: Performing exercises without proper guidance or instruction can increase the risk of injury or diminish the benefits of exercise.

It's important to approach exercise mindfully and with consideration of your individual circumstances. Consulting a healthcare professional or fitness expert can help you develop a safe and effective exercise plan tailored to your needs and goals.

Meditation

Meditation is a technique designed to train awareness and attention and achieve a state of calm. Meditation can be a free and accessible way to gain new perspective on dilemmas you are facing, manage your stress, increase awareness of your thoughts, feelings, and behavior, reduce negative thoughts and feelings, and increase gratitude.

One advantage of meditation is that it can be done in as little as a few seconds - deep breath in, deep breath out, feet flat on the ground - anywhere you are without drawing attention to yourself. You can meditate through mindfulness in the middle of a difficult conversation, while you are getting a root canal, or when you experience turbulence on your next flight.

Below are listed some of the top benefits of meditation for mental and physical well-being:

Stress Reduction: Meditation helps activate the relaxation response, reducing the production of stress hormones and promoting a sense of calm and relaxation.

Anxiety Management: Regular meditation practice can reduce symptoms of anxiety by teaching individuals to observe their thoughts without judgment and gain a better understanding of their inner experiences.

Emotional Regulation: Meditation enhances emotional awareness, allowing you to identify and manage your emotions in a healthier way, reducing emotional reactivity.

Improved Focus and Concentration: Meditation trains the mind to stay focused on the present moment, which can enhance your ability to concentrate and improve cognitive performance.

Mindfulness and Present Moment Awareness: Meditation cultivates mindfulness, helping you become more attuned to the present moment, fostering greater presence, and reducing excessive rumination.

Lower Blood Pressure: Mindfulness meditation has been linked to reduced blood pressure, promoting cardiovascular health and lowering the risk of hypertension-related issues.

Enhanced Immune System: Regular meditation can boost immune function, making your body more resilient against infections and illnesses.

Better Sleep: Meditation encourages relaxation and can improve sleep quality by reducing insomnia symptoms and helping you fall asleep more easily.

On the opposite hand, meditation does not produce the same positive results for everyone. A study conducted in 2017 found that some practitioners reported panic, hallucinations, reliving of traumatic experiences, and demotivation.

While meditation offers numerous benefits for mental, emotional, and physical well-being, it's not a one-size-fits-all solution and can have some shortcomings or challenges:

Difficulty Concentrating: Meditation often involves focusing on a specific object, breath, or mantra. For some people, maintaining this focus can be challenging, leading to frustration and a sense of failure.

Impatience and Expectations: People might expect immediate results from meditation, leading to impatience when they don't experience profound changes right away. This can hinder their commitment to consistent practice.

Time Commitment: Regular meditation requires a commitment of time and effort. People with busy schedules or those who struggle to set aside time might find it hard to incorporate meditation into their routine.

Physical Discomfort: Sitting or maintaining a specific posture during meditation can lead to physical discomfort or even pain, which can distract from the practice and make it less effective.

Resistance to Stillness: Some individuals have a hard time sitting still and being alone with their thoughts. This can lead to restlessness or discomfort during meditation sessions.

Overwhelming Emotions: As meditation encourages self-awareness, it can bring up suppressed or difficult emotions. This can be challenging to navigate without proper guidance or emotional support.

Cultural and Religious Concerns: Certain forms of meditation are tied to specific cultural or religious contexts. People from different backgrounds might have concerns about appropriateness or may not resonate with the cultural aspects.

Ineffectiveness for Some Issues: While meditation can help with stress, anxiety, and general well-being, it might not be as effective for certain mental health conditions. In some cases, professional intervention may be necessary or the use of alternative methods such as writing.

Initial Discomfort: Beginners might find meditation uncomfortable due to the unfamiliarity of stillness and self-reflection. This discomfort can discourage them from continuing the practice.

Cognitive Styles: Some people might have cognitive styles that make certain meditation techniques less suitable for them. For example, those who have highly active minds might struggle with practices that emphasize quieting their thoughts.

Lack of Guidance: Without proper guidance or instruction, individuals might struggle to grasp the nuances of meditation techniques, leading to a lack of progress or frustration.

It's important to note that these shortcomings are not universal, and many individuals find meditation to be a valuable and transformative practice.

Yoga

Yoga is a spiritual exercise that helps you establish and access the connection between your body and your mind. Over 36 million Americans practice yoga, making it a popular way to manage stress and improve health and wellness. Yoga offers several benefits:

- it can be done almost anywhere at any time with little to no equipment;

- it improves balance, strength, and flexibility;

- practicing regularly can alleviate back pain, chronic pain, and arthritis pain;

- it can provide an advanced level of relaxation, helping you manage stress and improve sleep;

- it can improve your mood.

Yoga offers a wide range of benefits for both the body and mind. Here are the top five benefits of yoga:

Improved Flexibility and Range of Motion: Yoga involves a variety of poses and stretches that help lengthen and stretch muscles, gradually increasing flexibility and enhancing range of motion in joints.

Enhanced Strength: Many yoga poses require you to support your own body weight, which can lead to increased muscle strength, particularly in the core, arms, legs, and back.

Stress Reduction and Relaxation: Yoga incorporates breathing techniques and mindfulness, which can lower stress hormones and promote a state of relaxation, reducing overall stress and anxiety.

Better Posture and Body Awareness: Yoga emphasizes proper alignment and body awareness, helping to correct and maintain good posture, reducing strain on muscles and joints.

Mind-Body Connection and Mental Well-Being: Through its emphasis on mindfulness and meditation, yoga can promote self-awareness, emotional balance, and a sense of overall well-being. It can also help with managing symptoms of anxiety and depression.

However, yoga also comes with limitations. Long-term, measurable benefits are realized with intentional practice three to five times per week. Each of these sessions lasts an hour on average. For those with full schedules, the time that yoga demands can be limiting.

While yoga offers numerous benefits, it's important to acknowledge its limitations as well. Here are the top five limitations of yoga:

Not a Substitute for Medical Treatment: Yoga can complement medical treatments, but it should not be used as a sole replacement for medical advice or treatment. Serious medical conditions require proper medical attention and consultation with healthcare professionals.

Physical Limitations: Some yoga poses might not be suitable for individuals with specific physical limitations, injuries, or medical conditions. It's important to practice under the guidance of a qualified instructor who can provide modifications and ensure your safety.

Complexity: Certain yoga practices and advanced poses can be complex and require a significant amount of time and dedication to master. This might discourage beginners or individuals with busy schedules.

Risk of Injury: Without proper alignment and guidance, there's a risk of injury in yoga, especially when attempting advanced poses or pushing beyond your physical limits. Practicing with an experienced instructor is essential to minimize this risk.

Limited Cardiovascular Benefits: While yoga offers benefits for flexibility, strength, and relaxation, it may not provide the same cardiovascular benefits as more intense forms of aerobic exercise like running or cycling.

It's crucial to approach yoga with awareness of your own limitations and to practice in a safe and mindful manner. If you have any concerns about practicing yoga, especially if you have underlying health conditions, it's advisable to consult your healthcare provider before beginning a new exercise routine. Additionally, choosing a style of yoga that aligns with your goals and physical condition can help you make the most of the practice while considering its limitations.

Additionally, while intermediate or advanced practitioners can transition to practicing anytime, anywhere, most yogis will need guided instruction for weeks, months, or years before they reach that level of proficiency. This instruction requires travel to a gym, paid membership, and additional time and commitment in many cases. For those with past or current injuries or restrictions, yoga may be out of reach altogether.

Finally, the yoga industry has been commercialized and monetized. The truth is that you can practice with very little, but the first time a yogi shows up to class, surrounded by $90 leggings and three-figure yoga mats, it can begin to feel like an exclusive club. As a result, the habit has the potential to become expensive and potentially detrimental to your self-esteem.

Medication

Medication is a valuable tool, often helpful in fighting the symptoms of depression, anxiety, and chronic stress. However, as those who take medication for *any* health condition know, there is not a single drug on the market that is not accompanied by side effects and the potential for serious adverse events. Only a patient and their healthcare team can determine when it is the right time to add medication to the proverbial toolbox: that is, when the benefits outweigh the risks.

Medications commonly used for the treatment of anxiety and depression include SSRIs, antidepressants, anxiolytics, sedatives, and nerve pain medications. In some cases, medications may also be used for chronic or situational stress.

Aside from the risk of side effects and adverse events, there are populations that do not have access to this tool when facing stress, anxiety, and depression.

Here's a breakdown of the benefits and risks of taking prescription medication for mental and physical well-being:

Benefits:

Symptom Management: Prescription medications can effectively alleviate symptoms of various mental health conditions such as depression, anxiety, bipolar disorder, and schizophrenia. They can also manage physical health conditions like hypertension, diabetes, and chronic pain.

Improved Quality of Life: By managing symptoms, medications can enhance your overall quality of life. They can help you regain functionality, participate in daily activities, and maintain relationships.

Quick Relief: Medications often provide relatively fast relief from acute symptoms. This can be crucial for individuals facing severe mental or physical distress.

Combination with Therapy: Medication can work in conjunction with therapy to create a comprehensive treatment plan. This is often referred to as a biopsychosocial approach, which addresses biological, psychological, and social factors.

Prevention of Complications: In some cases, medication can prevent further complications. For instance, diabetes medication can help manage blood sugar levels and reduce the risk of long-term complications.

Limitations:

   Side Effects: Prescription medications can come with side effects, ranging from mild to severe. Common side effects may include nausea, dizziness, weight gain, or sleep disturbances.

   Dependency and Tolerance: Some medications, especially those for mental health, can lead to dependency or tolerance issues, requiring higher doses over time to achieve the same effect.

   Interaction with Other Medications: Medications can interact with each other, leading to adverse effects or reduced efficacy. This risk is particularly relevant for individuals taking multiple medications.

   Withdrawal Symptoms: Stopping certain medications abruptly can lead to withdrawal symptoms. This is a concern for medications that affect brain chemistry, such as antidepressants or anti-anxiety drugs.

   Misdiagnosis: Incorrect diagnosis might result in the prescription of inappropriate medications, potentially worsening the condition or leading to unnecessary side effects.

   Overmedication: Overprescribing or polypharmacy (taking multiple medications) can increase the risk of adverse effects and interactions.

   Long-term Effects: The long-term effects of some medications are not always well understood. There might be concerns about potential health risks that emerge after extended use.

   Stigma: Some individuals may feel stigmatized or perceive a sense of weakness if they need to rely on medication for their well-being.

   Personal Resistance: Not everyone responds to medications in the same way. What works well for one person might not work as effectively for another.

Lifestyle Impact: Some medications might require lifestyle adjustments, such as dietary restrictions or avoiding certain activities or substances.

It's crucial to make informed decisions about prescription medication. This involves an evaluation by a healthcare professional, considering your medical history, current health status, potential risks, and benefits. Open communication with your healthcare provider and regular follow-up are important to ensure that the prescribed medication is effective and well-tolerated.

Journaling

Journaling is a form of expressive writing that involves documenting the events of your life, or writing about your feelings surrounding those events. Guided journaling provides benefits like helping you achieve goals, tracking your growth and progress, improving self-confidence, managing stress and anxiety, coping with difficult feelings and experiences, healing from trauma, and more. Journaling can be used to set and work toward goals, to document your fitness journey, to reflect on what went well at the end of each day, and more. As an added benefit, almost anyone can incorporate journaling into their routine in just five to fifteen minutes a day.

Journaling offers a wide range of benefits for personal growth, self-awareness, and emotional well-being.

Here are some of the key advantages:

Emotional Expression: Journaling provides a safe and private space to express your emotions and thoughts without fear of judgment. Writing down your feelings can help you process and understand them better.

Self-Reflection: Regular journaling encourages you to reflect on your experiences, actions, and decisions. This introspection can generate self-awareness and personal growth.

Stress Reduction: Putting your thoughts on paper can help alleviate stress. By externalizing your concerns, you may find that they appear less daunting, making it easier to manage them.

Problem Solving: Writing about challenges and concerns can help you analyze them from a more objective standpoint. This can lead to new insights and potential solutions to your problems.

Mood Regulation: Journaling can have a positive impact on your mood. Expressing gratitude and documenting positive experiences can boost feelings of happiness and contentment.

Clarity of Thought: Organizing your thoughts by writing them down can help clarify your ideas. This can be especially beneficial when making decisions or planning future actions.

Goal Setting: Journaling allows you to track your progress toward goals. Writing down your goals and the steps you're taking to achieve them can increase motivation and accountability.

Enhanced Creativity: Keeping a journal can stimulate your creative thinking. Freewriting, doodling, or exploring new ideas on paper can help you tap into your creative potential.

Memory Enhancement: Writing about your experiences can improve your memory retention. By detailing events, thoughts, and feelings, you create a record that can be revisited later.

Mindfulness: The act of journaling encourages you to be present and engaged in the moment. This mindfulness practice can lead to increased self-awareness and a stronger connection to the present.

Personal Insight: Over time, journaling can reveal patterns in your thoughts, behaviors, and emotions. This insight can lead to a deeper understanding of yourself and your motivations.

Catharsis: Writing about difficult experiences can provide a sense of release and relief. The act of acknowledging and sharing your feelings can be cathartic.

Empowerment: Journaling can help you regain a sense of control over your thoughts and emotions. It's a proactive way to manage your mental well-being.

Communication Skills: Regular writing can improve your ability to communicate clearly and effectively, as you practice articulating your thoughts and feelings.

The benefits of journaling are numerous and can be tailored to fit your personal goals and needs. Whether you're seeking emotional release, personal growth, or a tool for self-discovery, journaling can be a valuable practice to incorporate into your daily routine.

However, 'free' journaling comes with risks and limitations, too. Emotional distress, rumination, and lack of professional guidance can be concerns. Privacy, negative self-judgment, and pressure to write consistently are also limitations. Avoiding perfectionism and self-comparison is important. Balancing positive and negative aspects, seeking professional help if needed, and setting boundaries can make journaling more effective and mindful. It's a personal practice that should be adapted to individual needs. As discussed previously, when a journal is used to vent without the proper reflective elements, it can increase anger, stress, and anxiety.

Here are some potential limitations to consider:

Emotional Distress: Writing about difficult emotions or traumatic experiences can bring up intense feelings and potentially exacerbate emotional distress. It's important to gauge your emotional readiness and seek professional support if needed.

Rumination: Continuously focusing on negative thoughts or repeatedly writing about distressing events without seeking resolution might lead to rumination, where you're stuck in a cycle of negative thinking.

Privacy Concerns: If your journal is not kept private or secure, there's a risk of your personal thoughts and feelings being exposed to others, which could lead to embarrassment or breach of trust.

Negative Self-Judgment: Journaling might inadvertently reinforce self-criticism if you focus solely on your perceived shortcomings or negative events. Balancing this with positive self-reflection is crucial.

Pressure to Document Constantly: Feeling obligated to journal every day or to write eloquently might create unnecessary pressure, turning the practice into a chore instead of a helpful tool.

Perfectionism: Striving for perfect grammar, neat handwriting, or eloquent prose might hinder the raw expression that can be therapeutic in journaling.

Self-Comparison: If you compare your journal entries to those of others, you might feel inadequate or discouraged, missing the individuality of your own experiences.

Focus on Problems Only: If your journaling becomes solely focused on problems, you might overlook positive experiences or neglect gratitude and growth.

Time and Consistency: Regular journaling requires time and commitment, which might be challenging for some individuals with busy schedules.

Lack of Professional Guidance: While journaling can be therapeutic, it's not a substitute for professional help. Serious mental health issues may require the expertise of a trained therapist or counselor.

Ultimately, journaling is a personal practice, and finding what works best for you is essential. It's a tool that can be adapted and adjusted to meet your individual needs and preferences.

Rethinking Stress, Anxiety, and Search for Meaning

While we have an overwhelming number of options to consider when it comes to managing our difficult thoughts and feelings, none of them really address both stress/anxiety *and* search for meaning. None of them are suitable for all or even most people. Few are without risks.

It is time we rethink how we approach difficult thoughts and feelings using a process called guided, expressive writing.

CHAPTER 6

Lifewrite Writing Trails™

Like a walk in the woods or a morning meditation, Lifewrite Writing Trails take you on a journey. Each Writing Trail is designed to help you focus your attention on one area, analyzing your thoughts, feelings, and experiences in that topic, and then finding clarity and setting goals to guide your future. Let's talk about what we have learned throughout the previous chapters and how Writing Trails speak to each point.

Expressive Writing Leads to Health Benefits

In chapter two, we learned that writing about emotional experiences has several health benefits, including being associated with 1) a reduction in physician visits, 2) improved immune system function including antibody response and improved t-helper growth, 3) lower heart rate, 4) reduced phasic corrugator activity, and 5) long-term improvement in overall well-being and mood.

We learned in the same chapter that keeping secrets about trauma can be more damaging than having experienced the trauma.

Writing Trails answer the call here. They provide all the physical and emotional benefits of expressive writing and allow you to speak openly - in a safe and private setting - about difficult experiences. Because each exercise is guided, you can avoid the negative results that may occur when you write to vent and do not come full circle, challenging yourself to recognize growth and set goals.

Neural Pathways Drive Our Thoughts and Behaviors

We learned in chapter three that our thoughts and behaviors are influenced by neural pathways. That is, every time we have a thought, a pathway - like a trail through the woods - is formed. Inherently, our thoughts take the path of least resistance. That means that a negative thought gives birth to more negative thoughts.

Lifewrite Writing Trails guide you to create a new path in the woods by exploring new ways of thinking; ways of thinking that are more grateful, more thoughtful, more creative, and more healing than before. Each time you approach a situation from a new perspective, you make the first pathway through the woods. By repeating this process, subsequent times, you become more likely to take that path...the path that is kind to yourself, focused on your future, and grateful for this moment.

There is Science Behind What We Retain

We also learned in chapter three that there is science behind which information we retain and which information we discard on a real-time basis. What we retain is incredibly important. Retaining information not only sets us up for success at home, at school, and at work, but it also dictates what becomes our priority throughout the day. We learned in the same chapter that we are more likely to retain information that we generate ourselves and information that we memorialize in writing.

Lifewrite Writing Trails speak to both: when you complete a short Writing Trail, you generate new thoughts and ideas yourself, rather than reading or listening to somebody else's insights. By writing down your own thoughts, you also improve encoding and retention.

Delayed Return Stress Doesn't Serve Us

We learned in chapter four that stress was designed for immediate-return situations: threat > stress > action > positive outcome. In today's world, almost all of our stressors are not immediate threats, like a lion, tiger, or bear, but long-term threats, like inability to save for retirement or worry about raising kids in a challenging environment. Because these threats produce stress that does not lead to immediate action and immediate relief, the result is chronic stress and debilitating physical, emotional, and mental symptoms.

Writing Trails address stress in delayed-return situations by helping us explore action we can take in this exact moment to improve our long-term outcomes. Participating in these exercises can help you transition from an overwhelming long-term, big-problem perspective to a one day at a time perspective. It can take you from paralysis to action, encouraging small steps that lead to complete transformation in all areas of life.

The Search for Meaning Can Cause Dissatisfaction

In chapter five, we learned that the secret to finding your purpose is to stop looking for it and find it in the life you already have. It is common to go through the motions of everyday life without ever thinking about what it all means, but Lifewrite Writing Trails prompt you to stop and reflect, finding the meaning and purpose of the important connections you have made, challenges you've overcome, and work you've done. Rather than looking for meaning, you simply recognize all the meaning and purpose that you are already fulfilling mindfully every single day.

Doing is More Productive Than Thinking

We also learned in chapter five that a wonderful way to spend less time thinking about meaning, which is dissatisfying, is to spend more time doing the things that bring meaning and purpose into your life. Just as baby steps can help you address chronic stress by taking a step-by-step approach to long-term problems, Writing Trails can also help you establish positive micro-habits to get out of your head and into action.

Writing Trails can be completed in a single session or can be extended to last a week or longer. Supporting you with new daily primers with frequency to build new neural pathways. Creating an enhanced state of well-being is the objective and a key benefit of using Lifewrite.

Today's Solutions Have Shortcomings

In chapter six, we explored the shortcomings to some of the ways we approach growth, goal setting, stress, anxiety, difficult feelings, and situations experienced in today's world. Many solutions have been commercialized and monetized, often excluding those who have limited access, who live a minimalist lifestyle, or who simply do not have the resources to pay the entry fee.

At Lifewrite, core to our mission is to deliver both free and pay- for Writing Trails that serve the people of the world and their need to access solutions for the stresses and challenges of 21st century life.

Lifewrite Writing Trails are customized for your journey, strengths, and goals. Whether you have a budget or are looking for a free solution, our mission is to deliver to the world a new and easy to way to achieve mental and physical well-being through writing.

To become more immersed and focused in each Writing Trail, you can choose the relaxing background sound that speaks to you and choose whether to read the primers yourself or enjoy audio narration, making each exercise as inclusive as possible. By responding to each primer in writing – with no pressure to spell correctly or get the grammar or punctuation right – you generate the thoughts and ideas yourself and memorialize them externally, improving encoding and memory.

Lifewrite is an anywhere, anytime answer, whether you are processing daily stress, starting your day with intention and purpose, reflecting on the day before you go to bed, or planning for your future. Our goal is to help you take the first step toward transforming this moment, your day, and your future through writing. We are here, for you – to help you find clarity, set goals, work through challenging feelings, feel the highest level of gratitude, and become the best possible version of yourself.

Lifewrite is for everyone. For the healthy. For the struggling. For the successful. For the sick. For the challenged. For the vulnerable. For the powerful. And most of us are all of those, depending on the day, the year, the moment. At Lifewrite, we are here. We are here for you.

Start now by visiting us at Lifewrite.ai for updates and more information.

RESOURCES

The Write Way to Clarity
A Lifewrite Writing Trail™

Introduction

Many of us struggle with trying to figure out *what* we should be doing and *how* we should be doing it. There are so many conflicting priorities pulling us in different directions at all times. This pandemic has really made people question this even more, especially since when people finally had "extra time," so many of the things they thought they would do with that time simply did not get done.

So how do we figure out what we *want* to be doing, what we *should* be doing, and *when* we should be doing it? How do we ensure that we are not focused on the wrong things or putting our energy in places that they are not truly needed at the expense of not being present where we really are needed?

There is no overarching "right" response for everyone. As individuals, we all have different needs, different abilities, and different situations. So, while there may be no universal right or wrong, we do need to figure out what is right for *us* and what is wrong for *us*.

And one incredible way to figure out what is right is to write. Writing forces us to put the wide range of thoughts and feelings running through our minds and hearts into words. Each word is specific and when we choose a particular word over another, it helps us home in on what is most meaningful to us, what our priority is, and then we can see, literally on paper, what we are trying to understand.

This meditation, like all of the Lifewrite Writing Meditations, is intended to be done as often as possible. The more you do it, the more you will be able to track your progress and growth.

Remember the more you travel on the trail the more you are activating change in your destiny! We encourage you to always print out and keep a copy with the date of your writing meditations so that you can compare where you were to where you are now and where you want to be going.

Our meditations are intended to take no longer than 15 minutes. They are short, but focused and powerful. And they *will* make a difference.

Thank you for joining us on this journey to find clarity in your life!

Step 1:

Date: ____

Time: ____

Location: ____

Everyone has the things they have to do and then the things they want to do. Often the things we want get shoved to the side for lack of time, money, or ability. But it is vital we recognize them and see how they can be incorporated in our lives.

List the top three things that you have to do that occupy the majority of your time:

1.____

____

2.____

____

3.____

____

Now list the top three things that you would want to do if time, money, or ability wasn't standing in your way:

1.____

____

2.____

____

3.____

____

Step 2:

While clearly there are things that only we can do, there are often things that can be outsourced and can be done just as well (if not better) by someone else. When our energy is spent in areas that others could do for us, it leaves us depleted for the areas that we should be doing ourselves.

Of the three things you listed that you have to take care of, now write a list of three aspects of those areas that can be outsourced so that you can lessen the overall time and effort you must be putting into those areas:

1. ____

____

____

2. ____

____

____

3. ____

____

____

Step 3:

Now I want you to write three things you can start doing as of today that can get you more involved with or connected to the three things you want to be doing. For example, if you wish you had time to paint or work out, you could schedule 30 minutes at some point this weekend to work on that. If you wish you could travel but don't have time or money to do so right now, you could still plan something more local where you can get away, even if just for a few hours:

1.____

____

____

2.____

____

____

3.____

____

____

____

Step 4:

One really powerful way to help prioritize or re-prioritize what we are doing in our lives is to recognize the areas where we are replaceable and where we are irreplaceable. This can be eye-opening when we face the (sad) fact that no matter how high our position, if we were to leave, it would only be a matter of time before someone else could fill our shoes.

However, there is no one else who can be the daughter that you are, or the brother, or the friend, or the aunt, or the father, etc.

Write down who you are irreplaceable to in your life and who in your life is irreplaceable to you. Next to each person (or thing) write down if you feel you are spending enough time and energy with this person (or thing).

Who are you irreplaceable to: _______________________

____

____

Who is irreplaceable to you: _______________________

____

____

Are you spending enough time with this person: _______

____

____

Step 5:

This is your final step. For this step, you are going to time yourself and you will write for **five minutes only**.

For five minutes I want you to write about where you want to be and who you want to be five years from now. As you write, speak about it as if it is your reality. So rather than saying: "I want to be married" write "I am married to the love of my life, and we have a dog and two kids." Create your reality through your writing.

When you are done, read it aloud. And then ask yourself the foundational question:

"Are the three things that occupy the majority of my time (from Step 1), bringing me closer to where I want to be in five years? Or are my priorities keeping me from them?" Only *you* can answer that question. And only *you* can change your order of your current priorities!

Conclusion:

Figuring out your priorities and where to put your energy can be challenging, yet once there is clarity in this area, so many other things will fall much easier into place. It is vital to recognize that the focus needs to be on where you are putting your effort and what order you are working on. That doesn't mean that you won't be able to do other things or that you need to give things up, but rather they are not the most important things to take care of.

This meditation is intended to help you find that order of priorities so that you can know what you want to accomplish and create a plan to get there. We encourage you to hold onto your responses so that you can look back and see if you stuck with what you decided and if you want to keep moving in that direction or perhaps reprioritize. The more often you do this meditation, the easier it will become to recognize the issues, your negative patterns that need breaking, and putting your competing interests and responsibilities into the healthiest order for you to tackle.

The following questions will help us improve these meditations which will help you in your life!

Do you feel calmer and clearer after doing this meditation?

Yes or No.____

Why or why not?____________________________________

____

____

____

____

____

____

Thank you for taking the time to invest in yourself to find clarity in your life. We hope this leads to even more success as you move forward!

The Write Way to Sleep
A Lifewrite Writing Trail™

Introduction

We all need sleep. We all want sleep. But few of us get enough of it. Actually one in three people don't sleep enough on a consistent basis.

There are numerous approaches that aid with better sleep, but did you know that writing is one of them? A 2018 study by Baylor and Emory Universities found that fifteen minutes of writing immediately before hitting that pillow can decrease distraction, overthinking and worry, thus allowing you to sleep better.

This Lifewrite Meditation, Write to Sleep, will take you through a series of steps to help you process your day, plan for the coming day, reflect on the positive and tie up the loose ends so that when you finally lie down you can relax and focus on sleeping rather than all the things you have to take care of.

You don't need to be a writer to do this meditation. You just need to be willing to try writing as a method for better sleeping. When you start waking up feeling more rested and calm, you will know it is working!

Before we start, please put:

Date: ____

Time: ____

Location: _______________________________________

What time do you need to wake up?_____________________

How many hours of sleep do you hope to get tonight? ______

Step 1:

Do you ever get into bed, pull the covers up, only to remember something important you have to take care of? You might fear that if you don't write it down you will forget by the morning and you debate whether or not to get out of bed to do so.

So, the first thing I want you to do, is to create your "To Do" list for the morning. This list will then be something you can reflect on the following evening to determine what you were able to accomplish and what still needs to be done.

To Do List:

1. ____

2. ____

3. ____

4. ____

5. ____

____

____

____

____

Step 2:

Not only can we have a hard time sleeping when we are worried about what we need to do, but often we can't fall asleep because of something we have done that we regret.

For this step, I want you to write out three things that happened today that you wish you handled differently. Or if could be three things that happened to you that bothered you and you felt hurt or upset by. This is your chance to vent and get those negative feelings out so that you can clear your heart and mind to get a good night sleep.

Three things that I could have handled better or that hurt/upset me today:

1.____

____

____

2.____

____

____

3.____

____

____

Step 3:

Now is the time to reset and choose how you want to be tomorrow. Tomorrow is your opportunity to be better and do better.

Perhaps there are people you need to apologize to? Or maybe you need to set a time to speak to someone and let them know that their comment hurt you?

____

____

____

Write three things that you want to do tomorrow to have a more positive day and that will help put closure to what you did, or what was done to you today, that needs fixing:

1. ____

____

2. ____

____

3. ____

____

Step 4:

It can be easy to focus on the negative and forget the positive. But undoubtedly many things did work out well for you today and you managed to accomplish more than you might give yourself credit for.

For this step I want you to make two different lists. In the first list I want you to list five things you did today.

In the second list, I want you to write five things you are grateful for.

Five Things You Accomplished Today:

1.____

2.____

3.____

4.____

5.____

Five Things You are Grateful for Today:

1.____

2.____

3.____

4.____

5.____

Step 5:

Now, I want you to think of a reward for yourself tomorrow. Something you are going to put into your day to look forward to. You deserve it and have earned it and it will help you not only sleep tonight but look forward that much more to waking up and starting your day!

How will you reward yourself tomorrow for what you will accomplish?

____

____

____

____

CONCLUSION:

Thank you for doing this Write to Sleep Meditation. We hope it has helped you put things into perspective, reflect on your day, feel more prepared for tomorrow and have the right mindset both in what you will do when you are awake and to know you have worked through things in order to be able to sleep better tonight.

This is a meditation that can be done as often as you would like, ideally it can and should be done on a nightly basis. If you struggle with falling asleep or staying asleep, we highly recommend trying this for two weeks and then seeing the impact it will have on you.

Thank you for joining us and we hope you get a good night's sleep! Sweet Dreams!

The Write Way to Find Love:
A Lifewrite Writing Trail™

Introduction:

You've likely heard the famous Johnny Lee lyrics, "Looking for love in all the wrong places." And more often than not, that is exactly the situation. So many people are seeking a loving, healthy relationship but either are not sure where to find it, how to find it or how to keep it. But ultimately, if we don't know what we should be looking for, or what we want in a relationship, we won't even recognize when we have found it.

This Lifewrite Writing Meditation will help you determine what is most important to you in a relationship, how you are best able to contribute to a healthy relationship, what you can improve and if you are really looking in the right places for what you are looking for. If you are already in a relationship, this can help you clarify if it is healthy and perhaps where changes and improvements are needed.

This meditation will not take you longer than fifteen minutes. You may also choose from our Writing Sounds to provide you with a calm background for your writing.

Please fill out the following:
Date: ____

Time: ____

Current Relationship Status: __________________________

Where are you right now as you are working on this Lifewrite Writing Meditation?

____

____

____

Step 1:

Without thinking about it, I want you to write down the first five adjectives that come to your mind in response to the following question:

What qualities are most important to you in a relationship?

1. ____

2. ____

3. ____

4. ____

5. ____

____

____

Now, look at the list and, if needed, re-order them in order of importance to you (1 is most important, 5 is least important).

1.____

2.____

3.____

4.____

5.____

What are three non-negotiables for you in a relationship?

1.____

2.____

3.____

____

____

____

____

Step 2:

When you think about a healthy, stable, loving relationship, how would you order the following categories, 1-5, in importance (1 is most important, 5 is least)?

______Physical qualities (attraction, looks, body type)

______Material qualities (if the person is financially stable, career, home/cars, lifestyle)

______Emotional qualities (if the person is a good communicator, open with sharing feelings, stable with emotions, a good listener)

______Intellectual qualities (if the person is interesting, intellectually challenging or curious, intelligent)

______Spiritual qualities (the person shares similar beliefs as you do, finds a spiritual/religious connection important in their lives, would want to raise kids with this upbringing)

Question: Based on what you feel is most important, did the five qualities you previously chose align in Step 1 with the order you are now choosing?

____

____

____

____

Step 3:

The following list of qualities represent those that are considered the foundation of healthy, long-lasting, loving relationships.

Put a check next to each one of these qualities that you have already listed as important to you.

___Honest   ___Respectful   ___Patient

___Trustworthy   ___Communicative   ___Flexible

___Empathetic   ___Reliable   ___Appreciative

___Kind   ___Listens   ___Growth-oriented

For those without a check, which qualities resonate most with you that you should perhaps focus on either in addition to, or in place of, the qualities you prioritized?

____

____

____

____

____

____

Step 4:

When looking honestly at yourself, what are the five most important aspects or qualities that you feel you have to contribute to a relationship?

1. ____

2. ____

3. ____

4. ____

5. ____

What area or areas do you feel you need to work on and improve to be a healthier partner to another?

____

____

____

____

____

What is something you can do, starting today, to work on improving that aspect or aspects of yourself?

____

____

____

____

Step 5:

As important as it is to understand what we are looking for in a person and in a relationship, just as vital is determining if we are spending time in the places or doing that activities that will increase our chances at meeting someone.

For example, if you are looking for a serious, committed relationship, but spend most of your free time hanging out at the local bar or at the gym, is that really where you are most likely to find someone ready to settle down?

____

____

____

____

What types of activities or places do you feel the kind of person you would want to be with would be most likely to attend?

____

____

____

Do you currently spend time in those places?

____

What can you start doing to invest more of your time in the places where a potential partner is likely to be?

____

____

____

Conclusion:

The most important thing you can do in finding a healthy relationship, is knowing what you are looking for in a person before that first date. Once your emotions kick in, it can be really hard to see the red flags, no matter how glaring they may be! Never forget your non-negotiables and ensure that the qualities you deemed most important are the ones that this person really embodies.

We encourage you to save this and reflect back on it in the future. And keep doing this Meditation when you first meet someone and as the dating process begins to keep yourself in check!

The Write Way to Parent:
A Lifewrite Writing Trail™

There is nothing more joyful, stressful, fulfilling, overwhelming, rewarding and challenging than parenting. One of the biggest mistakes we often make is looking to others to determine how we are parenting, when ultimately, no one knows us or our children better than we do. The goal of this Lifewrite Writing Meditation is to help you clarify your goals in your parenting, your hopes and fears and a plan that will work for you and your children. There is no right or wrong, there is only what is best for your family.

This is intended to take no longer than fifteen minutes which is a break you most definitely deserve and a gift to yourself that will benefit your entire family.

Before you begin, we encourage you to choose from one of our Lifewrite Writing Sounds to give yourself some relaxing background sounds while you write. And please fill out the following:

Time: ____

Date: ____

Age /Name of Kid/s: ____________________________________

____

____

Location: (if you are in the closet or bathroom, put that down!)

Step 1:

Let's begin by addressing the elephant in the room. When you think of yourself as a parent, what is your biggest fear of what you are doing wrong? Don't overthink this, just start writing what you worry most about when it comes to your parenting of your children:

____

____

____

____

____

Step 2:

We are unfortunately our harshest critics and are tough on ourselves even though we are loving to our children. But our children are sponges who absorb all the messages we give, both to ourselves and to them. I know, I am piling on the guilt, but this is important. You can't call yourself stupid, ugly, lazy, etc. and then expect them to believe they are intelligent, attractive, and go-getters. The best way we can raise happy children is by being happy parents.

Write the first five words that come to mind when you think of how you want your children to feel about themselves. Here are a few words you can choose from, or come up with your own:

Loved	**Positive**
Appreciated	**Happy**
Supported	**Confident**
Respected	**Wanted**

Or your words:

1. ____

2. ____

3. ____

4. ____

5. ____

____

____

____

____

____

Step 3:

If your child told you they didn't feel one of these things, what advice would you give them or how would you respond to the statement:

"I don't feel that I am ___________________________________

____

____ **"**

Write your response to your child:

____

____

____

____

Step 4:

Now I want you to read the very same response you wrote to your child, and say it to yourself. Do you believe it? Do you feel the things you want your children to feel?

I want you to come up with something practical you can do today to work on improving where you feel you are most lacking.

Statement: I am lacking in feeling

____

____

____

____

____

Action: Today I am going to do the following to make my-self feel better in this area by:

____

____

____

____

____

____

Step 5:

For the next five minutes you are going to write a letter to your children. This is not something that you are going to give them (unless you want to) but for you to put into words the kind of parent you want to be for them and what you want and hope for them. Write for five minutes only and don't edit or analyze, just free write exactly what comes out. To ensure you only write for five minutes, set a timer!

You can start with the following:

____

____

____

____

____

As your parent, this is what I want to be able to give to you, instill in you and model for you:

____

____

____

____

____

As your parent, these are my biggest hopes and dreams for you:

____

____

____

____

____

____

____

____

____

____

____

Conclusion:

Thank you for taking this time for yourself and ultimately for your children. Everyone has their own journey and struggles in parenting, but everyone, in their own way, can make small yet significant changes to become a better parent. And now that you put your goals in writing, you have made them that more tangible and that much easier to accomplish.

We encourage you to save this Lifewrite Writing Meditation and reflect back on it. And do it every time you are feeling overwhelmed or insecure about your parenting. Please answer the following questions to help us better help you:

Do you feel you benefitted from this Lifewrite Writing Meditation? Yes or No

Would you do this particular Meditation again in the future?
Yes or No

Would you recommend this to another parent you know?
Yes or No

Can you describe in a few words how you feel after doing this Meditation?

____

____

____

____

Do you have any other suggestions or feedback that you would like to share with us?

____

____

____

____

____

____

____

____

____

Thank you again for joining us on the journey of The Write Way to Parent!

The Write Way to a Life of Gratitude:
A Lifewrite Writing Trail™

Introduction:

Gratitude changes everything. Numerous studies prove that when we appreciate what we have, it changes our perspective, mood, behavior and interactions with others.

In this Writing Meditation we want to help you create an attitude of gratitude for the things you may already appreciate in your life, and we want to help you recognize and be thankful for the "normal" in your life and help you see how the ordinary is truly extraordinary.

Studies show that journaling for just five minutes a day for what you are grateful for can enhance your long-term happiness by over 10%. (FOOTNOTE *(Emmons & McCullough, 2003; Seligman, Steen, Park & Peterson, 2005). So, imagine the impact you will have on your well-being if you increase the gratitude in your life to cover areas that until now you may have even resented.

Over the next fifteen minutes you will dig deep, put feelings into words and words on paper. By the end of this writing meditation, you will look at your life through a new lens, and that lens will be one that will bring you more joy, more appreciation, and more hope.

Please fill out the following:

Date: ____

Time: ____

Location: ____________________________________

____

____

Step 1:

I want you to focus on the most obvious things in your life that you are thankful for. What are the first 5 things that come to mind that you are grateful to have. Do not worry if they are "big" things or "small" things, you can put down your children or a cup of coffee. Just write whatever comes to mind immediately:

1. ____

2. ____

3. ____

4. ____

5. ____

Now for each of the five, write down a sentence describing why you are grateful for these five things and if you feel you adequately show and express that gratitude.

1. ____

2. ____

3. ____

4. ____

5. ____

Before moving on, I want you take a moment to recognize that without much time or effort, you were able to come up with five things in your life you already have that you are grateful for. That is, in and of itself, quite a gift. Think about how fortunate you are and how many people may have really struggled to think of five things in their life.

Step 2:

Unfortunately, it is a lot easier for most of us to complain than to compliment. To be negative rather than positive. And because of that we spend a lot more time focused on what we are not happy about than all the things we have to be grateful for. But in each and every challenge, there is still something that can be focused on that is positive. If you are miserable in your job, recognize how fortunate you are to have a job. If you hate your car that keeps breaking down on your, focus on the fact that many don't have a car in the first place.

For Step 2 I want you to write down five things that are difficult and challenging for you in your life right now, and immediately next to those five, to find that silver lining, something you can be grateful for within this difficulty:

Five Things That are Challenging:

1.____

2.____

3.____

4.____

5.____

Silver Lining Within These Five Things:

1. ____

2. ____

3. ____

4. ____

5. ____

Step 3:

Now focus on areas of your life that you might be quick to overlook. Pick a few of the options below, or come up with 3 things you should always appreciate that you might be quick to take for granted:

Examples:

I woke up this morning breathing, with the gift of another day to live.

I woke up in a bed, grateful to have a roof over my head and shelter and grateful that I did not have to sleep on the street.

I am accessing this writing meditation on either a laptop or cell phone. I am grateful that I have access to such technology (even if borrowed) to be able to do something like this.

I took a hot shower and am grateful for running water and the ability to keep myself clean.

I ate breakfast this morning and am grateful to have food as there are so many people in the world who are starving.

Three Things I am Grateful for That I haven't Thought About Before:

1.____

2.____

3.____

____

Step 4:

One of the most important ways to build gratitude in our lives is through the act of giving. When we focus on helping another, we immediately become appreciative of the gifts we have in our own lives.

Here are a few ideas of things you could start doing today to help someone else while bringing more gratitude into your own life. These are acts of kindness you could do for a complete stranger to bring a smile to their face and yours:

Buy the coffee/meal of the person behind you in the drive-through

____

____

____

Hold the door open for the next person entering the building, smiling and saying "hello" as they pass

---

Compliment someone and watch their reaction

Give a larger tip than normal to someone who has helped you.

Buy a few flowers and hand them to someone who passes you on the street, telling them you just wanted to brighten their day.

____

____

____

____

Pick one of the above or choose your own, write down what it is you are going to do today and why you chose this specific action. When you do it, pay attention to how it makes you feel and how the other person responds to your kindness.

What is a random act of kindness that you are going to do today for a complete stranger?:

____

____

____

____

____

____

Step 5:

To end this meditation, we are going to come full circle. Think again about the five areas of your life, people or situations that you are most grateful for. They may be the first five you chose in Step 1, or by now you may have others you will want to add or prioritize.

Write five actions that you can begin immediately to acknowledge the gratitude for these top five areas in your life. And then, immediately after concluding this meditation, make one of them happen!

Five things I am most grateful for:

1. ____

2. ____

3. ____

4. ____

5. ____

Five things I can do, beginning today, to express this gratitude:

1.____

2.____

3.____

4.____

5.____

Which one are you going to do today?

____

____

____

Conclusion:

Thank you for taking the time to do our Lifewrite Writing Meditation: The Write Way to a Life of Gratitude. Here is your opportunity to share with us your feedback and save this meditation so that you will always have it to reflect back on.

We have found that our meditations are most effective when done weekly over a period of time. That is the best way to get a sense of your development and improvement in any given area. But even if this is the only time you do this, we hope you have gained from the experience and that is has made you a more grateful person for the gifts in your life.

For more information on Lifewrite and to receive updates on our journey visit our site at:

www.lifewrite.ai

About the Author

Introducing "The Writing Code" by Arthur Gutch, a visionary author with fourteen years of experience working with writers, a lifelong love for books, and an entrepreneurial spirit that fuels his creations. In this enlightening book, Gutch unveils the hidden powers of writing, explores ancient civilizations' secret methods of personal empowerment, and offers a groundbreaking solution for millions suffering from mental and physical challenges.

Driven by an unwavering passion, Gutch has embarked on a mission to unlock the true potential of writing as a tool for achieving optimal health, well-being, and unparalleled performance in all aspects of life. With a global mindset, he aims to transform the way we deliver wellness, bringing immense positive change to those in need.

Utilizing AI as a catalyst for extraordinary breakthroughs, Gutch's vision and passion reach new heights in the pursuit of health, well-being, and spiritual ascension. *The Writing Code* presents new methods in the codification of writing, revolutionizing the way we use writing as an exercise for better health, while breaking a sweat becomes a thing of the past.

Prepare to be captivated by Gutch's riveting journey through the realms of literature, history, and personal growth. Seamlessly blending ancient wisdom with modern technology, he presents a new paradigm that unleashes the transformative power of words, enabling readers to rewrite their own destinies.

The Writing Code is not just a book; it is a roadmap to a life of vitality, purpose, and self-empowerment. Join Arthur Gutch on this extraordinary adventure and unlock a new dimension of personal achievement that lies within the very words you write.